ISBN 978-1-332-87782-9
PIBN 10299733

1 MONTH OF
FREE
READING

at

www.ForgottenBooks.com

By purchasing this book you are eligible for one month membership to ForgottenBooks.com, giving you unlimited access to our entire collection of over 700,000 titles via our web site and mobile apps.

To claim your free month visit:

www.forgottenbooks.com/free299733

The date shows when this volume was taken.

To renew this book copy the call No and give to the librarian

HOME USE RULES

All Books subject to recall

All borrowers must register in the library to borrow books for home use

All books must be returned at end of college year for inspection and repairs.

Limited books must be returned within the four week limit and not renewed

Students must return all books before leaving town. Officers should arrange for the return of books wanted during their absence from town.

Volumes of periodicals and of pamphlets are held in the library as much as possible For special purposes they are given out for a limited time

Borrowers should not use their library privileges for the benefit of other persons

Books of special value and gift books, when the giver wishes it, are not allowed to circulate.

Readers are asked to report all cases of books marked or mutilated

Do not deface books by marks and writing.

The University of Basle

Medal of Pope Pius II,
Founder of the University of Basle,
engraved by Andrea Guazzalotti

First painting in University Register

Inauguration of Basle University

The University of Basle

General Information
for foreign Students

Printed by Frobenius ltd. Basle

5

INDEX

View of Basle in the 18ᵗʰ century

Corner of Courtyard in the Townhall

I. BASLE AS A UNIVERSITY TOWN.

In the following pages we venture to call the attention of English speaking students to the advantages offered by the University of Basle in Switzerland. In doing so we believe to be serving the cause of that international goodwill and amity which it has been and is our natural function to plead and to promote by all the means at our disposal.

The Peculiar Character of Basle University.

Basle University having been founded in 1460 is by far the oldest of the Swiss universities. But her teachers have kept in close touch with the representatives of applied science, and moved onward with the rapid social and technical progress of time. It was the peculiar condition of the University that prevented her scholars from ever losing contact with men of practical experience. The University of Basle has always been maintained not by the country, nor by a canton, but by one small city. She became, as it were, the beloved foster-child of a small, but proud democratic republic. Her maintenance was felt to be a burden. But the more the burghers prospered by dint of hard work, trade and industry, the more they appreciated the peculiar lustre shed on the town by the University. They knew this lustre would last just as long as Basle continued to be a home of science and fine arts, not only a centre of business and industry.

One of the most striking items in the history of the University is the foundation of the Academical Society in 1835. It was a time of political unrest and financial trouble. The city-fathers for a moment lost heart and thought of abolishing the University. It was the business men who protested most loudly and claimed the privilege of placing the whole establishment on a sound financial basis. For this purpose they founded the Academical Society. They have stood god-fathers to the University up to the present day.

The Basle Theological Faculty was one of the first on the continent to train Protestant ministers and to send them abroad. In the early days of reformation there were intimate relations between the University of Basle and the British Evangelical divines, and the manuscripts in our archives testify to the lively correspondence carried on between the Basle teachers and their British disciples. Ever since those days the Theological Faculty has been looked upon as a mother by many outposts of the Evangelical Reformed Church in the far East and West, and has been conspicuous for teachers of unusual merit even in periods when the University as a whole had been put in the shade by younger rivals.

The success of the Chemical Industry at Basle, which was closely allied to the scientific research work of the University Scholars, gave a new start to the Chemical Section of the Faculty of Science.

To the manufacture of silk ribbons, started by French refugees, was added the manufacture of aniline dyes. The making of dyes led to the making of all sorts of chemicals, drugs, and pharmaceutical products, and in recent years the efficiency of the Basle Chemical works has attracted the attention of the old and the new world.

Likewise the development of the Geological Section is greatly owing to the practical application of its researches in the mining industry and in great engineering works. Dozens of our Science Graduates have of late been engaged by Dutch and British mining companies to explore the mineral resources in their oversea settlements, and have come back to their research work the better for the useful experience they gained.

II. GEOGRAPHICAL SITUATION OF BASLE.

The city of Basle lying at the northwestern corner of Switzerland, close to the French and German frontiers, is a spot where French and German languages and customs meet. Here the Rhine takes its decisive turn towards the North. Here the main railway lines converge which connect the ports on the English Channel and the North Sea via St. Gotthard and Simplon with Italy. Accordingly Basle is one of the most important points in Mideuropean traffic.

Basle as a Touring Centre.

Being less than a day's journey from every great capital or town of western or central Europe, Basle is conveniently situated for a man who wants to get acquainted with the chief places of Europe. Moreover, though situated at the extremity of Switzerland, it is within easy reach of all the Swiss districts, renowned for beautiful scenery. (cf. p. 19.)

III. THE LANGUAGE OF THE UNIVERSITY TEACHERS AND THE POPULATION.

The city and University of Basle being situated in the German speaking part of Switzerland, most of the lectures are held in German. Newcomers should, therefore, be acquainted with the German language, or at least, immediately after their arrival, make it their chief concern to learn German.

For beginners in German special preparatory classes are arranged by the University. The teachers are men experienced in the teaching of modern languages according to the most useful methods.

Basle is essentially a Swiss town. It is more than four hundred years since it severed its political, though not its intellectual connection with any of the continental empires. Just because it is a frontier-town, just because its population is day after day talking across the hedge to two powerful neighbours, it has stood its own ground, it has preserved its own personality much more jealously than many an inland town. Immigrants from the West and North were soon amalgamated, and their children became the staunchest supporters of the old democratic republican tradition.

Though in their daily intercourse the Bâlois, like all the German Swiss, stick to their dialect, their literary language is High German, which is spoken more purely by the higher classes than anywhere else in Switzerland.

IV. ADMISSION OF STUDENTS.

Students who only wish to follow certain lectures and exercises without graduating at the University, may get themselves registered as Hearers. As such they will enjoy all the advantages of the University and the institutions connected with it. Those Students who wish to qualify for a University degree must have been registered as matriculated Students. For this purpose they are required to present certificates indicating that they have attained a standard involving an education equivalent in their own country to that required for matriculation in the University of Basle. Swiss Students must have obtained a certificate of maturity either at a Grammar School, or at a Real School, or by passing a Matriculation Examination. Matriculation Examinations for Swiss and foreign Students are held twice a year, at the end of March and September.

British Students will be registered as matriculated students on presenting certificates of Matriculation for a British, or a British Colonial University, or a Polytechnical University, or certificates indicating that they were matriculated at a British University.

American Students will be registered as matriculated Students on presenting certificates indicating that they have been admitted to a First Grade University by a College Entrance Examination Board, or on presenting certificates indicating that they are Graduates of a First Grade University (B. A., Lit. B., or B. Sc.).

The different Faculties lay stress on certain points in order to ensure a successful pursuit of studies.

Students of Theology should have acquired a sufficient knowledge not only of Latin, but also of Greek. Moreover, candidates for Theological degrees should have satisfied their examiners in Hebrew.

The Faculties of Laws and Medicine demand that Students whose school-curriculum did not include Latin, should pass an additional examination in this subject.

Admission of Female Graduates.

Until now only women Students of Swiss origin and daughters of foreign residents at Basle have been admitted to University examinations. The admission of other foreign women Graduates is under consideration, and will, no doubt, be granted very shortly.

Women Students must have had the same preparation for all the Faculties as male Students.

V. EXPENSES.

A. Tuition and Examination Fees.

1) Tuition Fees vary according to the number of lectures for which a Student is registered. The average amount of Tuition Fees per Semester is

for Students of Theology, Arts, Science

from frs. 80 to 120 (£ 3 to 5, $ 16 to 24),

for Students of Chemistry from frs. 150 to 200 (£ 6 to 8, $ 30 to 40),

for Students of Medicine from frs. 200 to 300 (£ 8 to 12, $ 40 to 60).

2) Examination Fees, payable to the University, for admission to Examinations,

a) Fees for Intermediate Examinations in Theology and Medicine, from frs. 30 to 60 (£ 1.5 to 2.10, $ 6 to 12).

b) Fees for Final Examinations, including Doctor's degree,
in the Faculty of Theology, frs. 100 (£ 4, $ 20),
in the Faculty of Laws, frs. 350 (£ 14, $ 70),
in the Faculty of Medicine, frs. 300 (£ 12, $ 60),
in the Faculty of Arts, frs. 325 (£ 13, $ 65),
in the Faculty of Science, frs. 325 (£ 13, $ 65),

B. Board and Lodging.

Foreign Students generally reside in lodgings, with, or without board. Registers of suitable lodgings are kept at the University Registrar's (Universitätspedell), and may be consulted by Students. The rent for single furnished rooms is from frs. 25 to 50 (£ 1 to 2, $ 5 to 10) per month, for double rooms from frs. 50 to 100 (£ 2 to 4, $ 8 to 20) per month.

The average price for Board and Lodging, single room, per month is from frs. 150 to 200 (£ 6 to 8, $ 30 to 40), double room, from frs. 225 to 250 (£ 9 to 10, $ 45 to 50).

Students who think it more convenient to have breakfast and supper at home, and dinner at a refreshment room, will be served good dinners at Temperance Hotels at fr. 1.50 (15 d, 30 cents). Foreign Students are strongly recommended to give the preference to pensions where boarders are received as members of the family. Addresses of such pensions with all necessary particulars will be given by the University Registrar.

It may be safely asserted that, even taking into account the actual conditions, Students can manage to live comfortably during the Sessions, and have their due share of healthy recreation in vacation time, on frs. 4000 a year (£ 160, or $ 800).

For Students who have had a sound grammatical training, and who have some experience in teaching, there is always a chance of contributing to their own support by giving private lessons in English.

VI. CONSTITUTION AND ADMINISTRATION OF THE UNIVERSITY.

There are five Faculties in the University, namely: (1) Theology, (2) Laws, (3) Medicine, (4) Arts, (5) Science. [(4) and (5) go under the old names, Philosophy First Section, Philosophy Second Section].

The University as well as the other educational establishments are maintained by the municipality of Basle and supervised by the Board of Education.

The financial and legal administration of the University is in the hands of the Curatel (Trustees), a body of five men chosen by the cantonal government from among professional and lay citizens of the town.

The supreme governing and executive body of the University is the Regenz (Senate), a council comprising all the appointed University professors.

The teaching staff of the University consists at present of 55 professors ordinarii, 35 professors extraordinarii, 45 privatdozenten, and 10 lectors.

The Rector of the University and the Deans of the Faculties are elected by the professors for the term of a year.

Professors are nominated by the Board of Education and appointed by the Cantonal government.

Professors ordinarii are appointed to hold the regular lectures and exercises which are prescribed in the various Faculties for the course of studies to be followed to obtain a degree.

Professors extraordinarii hold, as a rule, additional lectures and exercises not prescribed by the Examination Regulations.

Privatdozenten are young savants who wish to qualify for the academical career, and who have given sufficient proof of their aptitude for high class teaching and research work.

Lectors are assistant teachers whose chief work consists in supplementing by practical exercises the theoretical lectures of the professors ordinarii.

VII. SESSIONS.

The teaching year of the University is divided into two Sessions, or Semesters. The first, or Summer Semester, begins in April and lasts without any interruption until the middle of July. The Midsummer vacation lasts three months.

The Winter Semester lasts from October till March, with a break of two weeks at Christmas.

VIII. UNIVERSITY ADVANTAGES.

For the use of University Students there is a great number of auxili-ary Institutions, such as libraries, seminars and special institutes.

The University Library has swallowed up a goodly number of smaller libraries of ancient and modern date, and is now installed in a large and commodious building. Each Seminar and Institute affiliated to the Uni-versity has a library of its own with comfortable reading rooms.

An other exceedingly well stocked library is that of the Lesegesell-schaft (Reading Club). It is open to Students at a reduced fee. It is espe-cially designed to suit the lovers of modern German, French, English, and Italian literatures.

Students who are anxious to make the most of their time and the opportunities offered for professional research work, should join the Seminars, i.e. the special training schools of the various Faculties, where a limited number of qualified Students are initiated into the methods and problems of scientific work.

There are Seminars for Theology, Laws, Pedagogy, Classical Philo-logy, Archaeology, Comparative Philology, German, French, English Philology; History, History of Art, History of Music, Political Economy, Social Administration, Mathematics.

The Study of Medicine and Natural Science is served by a large number of Special Institutes. They contain laboratories, work-rooms, reference-libraries, and are placed at the disposal of professors, who, with their assistants, train undergraduates and graduates in experimental work, and advise advanced Students in their investigations and researches.

Special Institutes are provided for Physics, Astronomy and Meteoro-logy, Chemistry, Chemical Physiology, Practical Chemistry, Pharma-cology, Mineralogy and Petrography, Geology and Palaeontology, Geo-graphy, Botany, Zoology, Physiology, Hygienics, Pathological Anatomy.

Advanced Students may, on fulfilling certain conditions, apply for special facilities in the use of the collections of museums and special institutes.

The Medical Clinics are integral parts of the various departments of the great Municipal Hospital. As patients are not only received from the town and the immediate vicinity, but from the neighbouring districts of France and Germany, for which Basle is a natural metropolis, there is an abundant supply of very interesting and even rare cases.

There are Clinics for Interior Medicine, Surgery, Otology, Laryngology, Ophthalmology, Diseases of Children, Dermatology, each of them connected with clinical wards and dispensaries.

IX. BASLE AS AN EDUCATIONAL CENTRE.

It is well known to all those who, before the war, had opportunities of enquiring into the state of education on the continent, that in all the points that used to make German scholarship an object of high praise, Basle, above all for its upper schools and its University, was placed on a level with the most advanced educational centres of Germany. Indeed, it was quite natural for Basle, the democratic city-republic, situated at the entrance to France and Germany, to compete with her western and northern rivals in sound learning and practical efficiency.

She could only attain this purpose by watching most carefully over the schooling and training of her rising generation, by providing for the most competent teachers, by endowing most liberally all her educational establishments.

How far the University succeeded in holding a place of eminence may be gathered from the fact that during the past fifty years ever so many of her professors were directly called away from Basle to the most renowned universities on the continent, and that certain professorships at Basle University were looked upon as the safest stepping-stones to the very highest appointments in their line, and that, consequently, these professorships were generally held by men who left their mark in the history of science. It may be safely stated that whatever was good and worth imitating in German scholarship may be found at Basle too.

X. GENERAL TONE OF UNIVERSITY LIFE.

As the University of Basle has for four centuries and a half shared the fortunes of the city by which she was fostered, it is but natural that in her character she should faithfully reflect the character of the city and its population. As to the number of Students, Basle University was outdone not only by many younger universities of the continent, but even by her very young sisters of Zurich and Berne. But Basle University always took pride in being considered a place where Students were expected to take life seriously, to make good progress in their studies, and not to neglect their social training. The limited number of Students enabled the professors to get into close touch with all the members of their classes, to give them more personal help, and to live on more friendly terms with them than they could have done in places with crowded lecture-rooms.

XI. THE SOCIAL CHARACTER OF BASLE.

Basle is not a holiday resort, nor is it a town where pleasure and amusement prevail. The population of Basle is known to be earnest, thrifty, laborious. Young men who idle away their time, and are bent on wasting their father's money, are looked at askance at Basle. Because the prosperity of the population is due to the fine business qualities and steady habits of the manufacturers, merchants, bankers, young men are expected to cultivate those qualities that are conducive to health and happiness in later life.

Business and learning, hard work and noble enjoyment have for centuries been closely united here. Very often business and science were united in one person, more often in members of the same family. This narrow relationship between application to workday duties and application to fine arts has produced the tone peculiar to Basle Society and all its social gatherings.

We know from long experience that British and American friends have always felt at home here.

XII. HEALTH.

From a hygienic point of view Basle may be said to be a thoroughly modern city. In the second half of the nineteenth century, when the fortifications were pulled down, and healthy suburban dwellings spread far out into the country, various radical changes were carried out which greatly added to the salubrity of the town. The death rate of Basle is lower not only than that of most European towns, but than that of all other Swiss towns. This may be partly owing to the purity of the drinking water. The gravel and sand strata of the Rhine valley form an excellent filter for the subsoil water which supplies the water-works in the vicinity of Basle. The whole town is provided with a carefully controlled drainage-system. Most of the streets are macadamized and treated with tar.

The supply of provisions and their official control is well organized. Besides the systematic checking of the water supply, the analyses at the laboratory of the cantonal analyst extend to all food stuffs. The control of all butcher's meat, whether furnished from Switzerland, or imported

Wing of University Library

Banking House in Basle

from abroad, is carried out at the municipal slaughter-house where all animals, whether for public or for private use, must be slaughtered.

XIII. CLEANLINESS OF DWELLINGS.

In the plateau on which Great Basle is situated, a tributary of the Rhine has cut a deep valley along which the main streets of the city extend for about a mile. They have partly retained their ancient character, dating from the sixteenth and seventeenth centuries. In this low lying part of the city most of the business is carried on. Here there are three market squares, large shops and warehouses, numerous banking houses, the Stock-Exchange, the Central Post Office, the Town Hall, the Theatre, the Historical Museum, the Art Gallery, the Casino Concert Halls, and many hotels and restaurants. Although life is brisk in these business-streets, all the other parts of the town are remarkably quiet and nice to live in. The old houses in the centre of the town are either gradually being renovated, or entirely removed by virtue of an Inhabited House Act passed in 1907. The sacrifices incurred by the Municipality in this respect amount to many millions of francs.

Whatever difference there may be in social position and comfort between the richest and the poorest of the population, the dwellings of the poorer classes cannot even be distantly compared with the dismal workmen's quarters in the large manufacturing towns of other countries. Want and unthriftiness were ever rare among the inhabitants of Basle. All the streets are equally well lighted and swept, and within easy reach of the tramways. In all the services carried on by the State the principle of equality among all classes is rigidly enforced.

The older parts of the town are surrounded by extensive and well kept pleasure grounds which were laid out in the place of the former fortifications. Far beyond these promenades extend the new quarters, with straight broad streets and pretty villas, mostly single houses with gardens, whereas tenement barracks are rather rare.

Thus it is that the city covers a very large area in proportion to its population (140,000). Several of the modern quarters consist almost exclusively of handsome and even sumptuous villas with extensive gardens and lawns. The main features of the city may be said to be comfort and tranquillity.

XIV. THE ENVIRONS OF BASLE.

A glance at the map of Switzerland shows that the city of Basle is situated in a district highly favoured by nature.

It has grown up at the most important bend of the Rhine, where it still preserves much of its alpine freshness and youthfulness. It is guarded by three mountain ranges, the Jura, the Black-Forest, and the Vosges. In whatever direction one turns one's eyes, one may behold the blue wood-clad ridges of finely shaped hills, the lower spurs of which extend to the very outskirts of the city.

Both in summer and in winter, whenever the sun lights up the spires of the village-churches, and the towers of the frowning old castles, one feels tempted to stroll out into the country to have a look at those quaint old hamlets and sequestered townlets seen or guessed at from the distance.

For weeks at a stretch one may walk within a radius of a few miles from Basle, always meeting with new aspects of idyllic scenery. Moreover, a country, trodden by various nations for thousands of years, is sure to be full of reminiscences of all the past centuries.

Take for instance the Birs valley, the end of which has been turned into one continuous row of nice suburban villages. Before one has walked six miles, one will have come to the gates of half a dozen castles, some in a good state of preservation, some crumbling to ruins. In another direction one will within an afternoon's walk meet with the ruins of a frontier stronghold, erected after the designs of Vauban, the fortress builder of Louis XIV, and only half a mile off, towering high above a steep cliff, a picturesque convent and a grotto with a miraculous image of the Madonna, which is still venerated by Roman Catholic worshippers.

Numerous railway lines help to open up the neighbouring country, and a net of electric tramlines, starting from Basle, has been laid across the adjacent districts, so that a man fond of pedestrian tours is easily carried to the foot of the hill he wants to climb or traverse, and need not waste his time on the intervening space which may have no attractions for him.

Week-end Journeys.

A week-end journey will suffice to bring a visitor to the spots renowned for their historic associations and their landscape charms, such as the confluence of the Aar, Reuss, and Limmat rivers, where the cradle of the Hapsburg dynasty stands, or the shores of the Lake of Bienne, the favourite haunt of J. J. Rousseau, or the places of Middle and Lower Alsace, where one may see the finest and boldest fortified castles that were ever built by mediaeval lords or robber-knights.

Mountaineering Excursions.

Those Students who come to Switzerland with the desire as soon as possible to stand on one of the famous Alpine peaks and survey one of the huge panoramas in the Alpine regions, should bear in mind that a railway journey from three to six hours is needed to reach one of the places from which ascensions are usually undertaken.

If one starts from Basle on a Friday evening, one may, for instance, ascend the Jungfrau, return to Basle, and be ready for work again on Monday morning.

We would advise lovers of mountaineering to join the Students Section of the Swiss Alpine Club, and not to start on a trip, before they have made friends with one of the many Swiss Students who can look back on a long experience in mountain climbing, and who cannot only teach them how to avoid unnecessary dangers, but also unnecessary mistakes and useless expense.

These few hints should have made it clear that Basle, though it deserves recommendation above all on account of its traditional love of work and earnest living, is quite as attractive for its opportunities of healthy sport.

XV. SPORT.

There was a time when sports were little in favour with continental University Students. Most of their time was taken up by book and laboratory work, and for the rest of the day they indulged in too much idle pastimes and silly drinking bouts. We are happy to say that during the last thirty years a great improvement has taken place. British and Swiss sports have been taken up by most young men, and in Switzerland the University Students play a leading part in this healthy movement. The superiority of the Anglo-Saxon mode of life has been recognized by all the friends of youth, and the experiences of the last years have dealt the finishing blow to many obsolete traditions and habits.

Fencing is still by many considered a means of developing manly qualities. There is a fencing hall and a fencing master for the University Students at Basle.

Students may join the Academical football, hockey, and lawn tennis clubs.

In winter skating is a favourite pastime, but skiing has found most favour with young men and women. Indeed, it is asserted by devotees of

Basle Cathedral from the Quadrangle

In the Cathedral Cloisters

this art that it is not only the healthiest outdoor exercise, but that it opens up beauties of the hills and mountains such as no tourist ever beheld in his summer excursions.

There are several first class bathing establishments on the banks of the Rhine. There are also good opportunities for rowing.

During the week-ends and in vacation time lovers of aquatic sports may for a time remove their quarters to the lakes of Lucerne or Zurich.

XVI. SHORT DESCRIPTION OF THE CITY OF BASLE.

The Rhine which here, at its bend toward the North, has a breadth of 650 feet, and is 785 feet above sea level, divides the city into two parts, Great Basle on the left bank, and Little Basle on the right. Little Basle lies on level ground, pointing, as it were, to the level regions lower down the river. Great Basle with its rising hills forms a sort of transition to the hilly and mountainous parts of Switzerland.

The left bank of the Rhine on which Great Basle is built, rises sheer above the river, and high above it, built on a spacious terrace, towers the Cathedral with its two slender steeples. Stately patrician mansions are studded along the edge of the plateau, looking down with a noble calm on the rushing waves of the Rhine. This plateau with the Cathedral in its centre, offers a charming view, whether seen from the embankment on the other side of the river, or from one of the bridges, most charming when seen from the so-called Letzi tower.

The Cathedral.

The most impressive edifice is the Cathedral which dominates from its commanding position the ever growing assemblage of streets and lanes. One of its most conspicuous portions, the Gallus Porch, has the form of a Roman triumphal arch, and is an imitation of the Porte Noire at Besançon. Romanesque are all the portions of the structure that were conceived and carried out before the end of the thirteenth century, the Crypt, the broad central Nave, and the lofty pillars, the circular windows, the choice decorative friezes, besides the ground plan and the main vaults of the beautiful cloisters, connecting the church with the residence of the Bishop and Chapter. All the parts of the super-structure which are of a later date, are in the Gothic style, the façade, the steeples, incorporated in the main body of the church, after the earth-quake of 1356, and all the decorative traceries of the windows and arches.

City Gates.

Among the Gates which have survived the unmerciful modernizing tendencies of the nineteenth century, there is one that is to be seen in many picture-books as the most striking representative of mediaeval city gates. It is the Spalen Gate, built at the beginning of the fourteenth century, and decorated, in 1473, with a front structure and graceful statues.

XVII. ART AND SCIENCE.

Intellectual life has progressed hand in hand with material development. Evidence of this is to be found in the numerous museums, institutions, and collections, in a network of societies and organisations for the promotion of the public welfare. Both the intellectual and the material sides of life have always been strengthened and refreshed by the twofold influence of France and Germany.

The Art galleries of Basle and Geneva contain a number of wonderful paintings of the fifteenth century executed by a man whose unusual merit was only realized in recent days. It was Conrad Witz, a native of Constance, who came to Basle at the time of the Church Council and here, among other works, carried out a large covered altar, parts of which are preserved in the Art gallery. Whereas his predecessors had painted what they felt, Witz painted what he saw, and he knew how to paint it. Like the brothers Van Eyck in the Netherlands, he paved the way for a new line of art on the Upper Rhine.

The growing wealth and independence of the citizens, the sojourn of so many scholars and princes of the Church during the Council, brought about a love of splendour and a refined taste in dress and living which were bound to exercise a favourable influence on art and artists.

Not only the churches and guild-halls, but also tradesmen's houses were furnished with fine carvings, tapestries, stained glass, and costly furniture. A rare specimen of the art of this period is the Tschekken-burlin room in the Charterhouse (now Orphanage). Most strikingly, however, was the feeling of the growing power of the burghers expressed in the Town Hall which was entirely rebuilt between 1508 and 1520. The best artists were employed to carry out the architectural work and the external and internal decorations.

Hans Holbein.

To this city, teeming with intellectual and artistic life, came Hans Holbein, in the year 1515. At first he was employed at the studio of Hans Herbster, where he had to make drawings for wood-carving, ordered by the great Basle printers, and thus he gradually developed his brilliant gifts. From Lucerne where he had to decorate a nobleman's house, he proceeded to Italy, and returned to Basle in 1519. With his mind full of happy inspirations of the South, he executed a number of tasks entrusted to him by his Basle patrons. He painted the portrait of Boniface Amer-

bach, the learned jurist, collector, and patron of arts. Of his frescoes in the Town Hall only the original water sketches and later copies
are preserved. To this period belong the Passion, the Last Supper, several
Madonnas, the finest of which is the Darmstadt Madonna the sketches for
which, as well as for numerous portraits of English worthies at Henry VIII's
court are in the possession of the Art Gallery. Proofs of his exuberant
fancy are the numerous sketches for stained glass, the drawings for the
Dance of Death. When the troubles caused by the Reformation began
to interfere with his trade, Holbein emigrated from Basle to London. He
had been recommended to Sir Thomas Moore, Chancellor of King
Henry VIII, by Desiderius Erasmus, whose portraits he had so often painted
for his admirers in all parts of Europe. In vain did the Basle government
try to retain the artist by giving him important commissions. In 1529
the Reformation was followed by a violent democratic upheaval and
iconoclastic riots. For some time the Muses turned their back on Basle.
Holbein once more sought his fortune in England. At the Steel Yard he
obtained work from the Hansa merchants, and when the attention of Queen
Anne Boleyn had been drawn to him, he was appointed court painter to
Henry VIII. What treasures he left in the Halls and Galleries of England
is too well known to every English student to be repeated here. Only
in 1535 did he return to Basle for a short time, a grand seigneur, clad
in silks and velvets. But when he was snatched away by the plague in
London, only a pittance was left to his poor widow and children, whose
sorrowful portraits with their tearstained eyes remain to us as a pathetic
remembrance of Holbein's love of truth.

After Holbein, till far into the nineteenth century, no first rate artist
appeared at Basle. But Holbein's style dominated for a long time the
industrial art, especially stained glass. The Basle goldsmiths, too, kept
up Holbein's tradition until the eighteenth century.

Boniface Amerbach by Holbein

Desiderius Erasmus by Holbein

Jacob Burckhardt.

Another epoch of great artistic aspirations begins about the middle of the nineteenth century. This epoch was dominated by the genius of one of the most renowned citizens of Basle, Jacob Burckhardt, the great professor of Universal History and History of Art at the Basle University (a Swiss Ruskin), whose books on Italian art and Italian culture are known as standard works throughout the world. The best of the modern Swiss poets are imbued with his spirit, such as C. F. Meyer, J. V. Widmann, C. Spitteler.

Arnold Böcklin.

It is not a mere coincidence that a first rate painter arose from this milieu, Arnold Böcklin (1827 to 1901). In those of his paintings that he executed after he had found his own style, one may gather from the subjects he chose, and the manner in which he treated them, that in the depth of his soul he was at one with the master minds of old Greece and the Italian Renaissance. His Frescoes in the Staircase of the Basle Art Gallery (The Birth of Venus, Flora blessing the Earth, Helios.), his canvases in the same Gallery, the Naiades, the Centaurs, the Sacred Grove, etc., as well as his Pietà are, as it were, wonderful pieces of classic poetry expressed in colours. In power of imagination and brilliancy of colouring he certainly comes very near indeed to the great masters of the Italian Renaissance, and yet he is intrinsically Swiss.

Architectural Features of the City.

As to the architecture of the buildings, the Gothic style held the ascendancy until the second half of the sixteenth century. Then the spirit of Renaissance, inspired by noble Italian models, produced such delightful structures as the Spiesshof, built at the expense of a famous Dutch refugee, and the Geltenzunft (Vintner's Guildhall).

Visitors to the Historical Museum will not fail to admire a series of rooms the furniture and stained glass of which was removed there from guildhalls and private mansions. Since the middle of the eighteenth century a new impulse was given to the development of architecture at Basle. The prosperous families vied with each other in erecting spacious mansions in French Renaissance style. And, strange to say, it was the town-residence of a neighbouring princelet, the Margrave of Baden (it has since become the nucleus of the Municipal Hospital) that caused the rich burghers to overcome their conservative tendencies, and, if possible, to compete with the outsider in showing off their wealth in the noble façade and proportions of their mansions.

This new start in architecture brought to perfection a long neglected branch of art, that of decorative blacksmith work. Wrought-iron gates, balconies, and window-gratings, sometimes of the most exquisite workmanship, lend a peculiar grace to many a building in a quiet street or lane.

At the present day Basle is still an unusually fertile ground for artists, especially painters and musicians, which is not to be wondered at seeing that there are so many facilities to encourage and develop talented young men of an artistic bent of mind.

XVIII. ART AND SCIENCE COLLECTIONS.

The nucleus of the Scientific Collections at Basle was the Art Cabinet of the Amerbach family, which contained treasures and curios of the most various kinds, paintings, medals, coins, furniture, marvels of natural science. It was purchased by the State in 1662, and in course of time, other private collections were added. But the Museum, built in 1849, soon proved too small for the ever increasing collections, and separate premises had to be found for most departments.

First and foremost stands the Public Art Collection which is still a department of the University. It includes a rich cabinet of copper-plates, and a choice collection of drawings and wood-carvings. Nowhere can the Student of Art study to more advantage the older schools of painting and their periods of evolution than here.

Historical Museum.

The Historical Museum was originally a University Institute. It is conspicuous for its rich collection of house furniture, church-antiquities, glass and metal ornaments, massive silver and gold plate. It has a three-fold object: it collects everything that possesses historical importance for the city of Basle and its neighbourhood; it serves as a school of instruction for modern industrial art; it is an indispensable armoury for the archaeologist and the historian.

Natural History Museum.

The growth of the Natural History Museum is closely allied with the names of prominent scientists of Basle. The geological, mineralogical, and palaeontological collections recall the names of Peter Merian and Ludwig Rütimeyer, two men who for decades were supreme in Switzerland for all geological and palaeontological researches.

Ethnological Museum.

The Ethnological Museum deserves special mention. To accommodate the vast stores of new finds and treasures brought home by travellers in foreign lands, new wings were added to the Old Museum, in which the visitor will find, tastefully exhibited and carefully classified, most valuable materials from all the continents.

Particularly interesting are the collections brought from the islands of the Indian and the Australian archipelagoes by Messrs. F. and P. Sarasin, and from Africa by Messrs. David and H. Vischer.

A most attractive section of this Museum is the Swiss Ethnological Collection. Here one may trace all sorts of objects used by man, woman and child from the days of primitive mankind down to the epoch when modern civilisation invaded and refined the habits of the remote and sequestered valleys of the Alps.

Art Exhibitions.

Exhibitions of modern painters are held all the year round in the rooms of the Artists Club. At the opening of the Exhibitions introductory lectures are held by an expert.

Sculpture Hall.

In the Sculpture Hall there are plaster-casts of the Classical statuary of ancient and modern times serving for object-lessons to Students of Archaeology and History of Art.

Arts and Crafts School.

The Arts and Crafts School has a well arranged system of day and evening classes for Drawing, Sketching, Painting, Carving, Modelling, and all kinds of Manual Work needed by proficient mechanics and handicraftsmen. All these classes are open to University Students as well as to professional students and apprentices.

The School is combined with an Industrial Museum with a library and reading-rooms for the use of internal and other Students.

Scientific Societies.

Great is the number of Societies formed for the Promotion of Science, where professional and unprofessional men meet for the purpose of giving and receiving instruction, and communicating the results of their private studies and experiments. At their meetings papers are read by academic teachers and dilettanti, followed by discussions.

XIX. MUSICAL LIFE.

There is hardly a university town on the continent where a lover of music has so many opportunities of hearing first rate performances of classical music, and of perfecting himself in all branches of vocal and instrumental music. So dear has music been to the citizens of Basle for many centuries that it is considered an integral part of good breeding to be well versed in music. Accordingly music is an important item in the educational programme not only of the upper classes, but of the board schools. There is no end of glee-choirs, choral societies, bands etc. Even the working classes want to have their musical clubs. The concerts of the high class choral societies such as the Gesangverein, the Liedertafel, the Bach Choir are musical events not only for Basle and Switzerland, but for the neighbouring parts of France and Germany too. The great Spring Concerts of the Gesangverein and the Orchestral Society to which the first stars in the musical world of the continent contribute their share, make the hearers acquainted with all the great musical compositions of the Past and Present.

The University Students too have formed an Academical Orchestral Society whose performances have been highly appreciated by the public, they generally lend their services to the embellishment of University Functions.

It is owing to an excellently organized School of Music and Conservatoire that so many young men and women with a talent for music can be trained for the performance of high class music. The School is also open to foreigners.

XX. THEATRE.

The Municipal Theatre is much patronized by University Students. Its performances of classical and modern plays and operas are considered as a necessary contribution to the understanding of literature and social evolution. As companies of French players frequently visit the city of Basle, lovers of the French language and dramatic art will also be able to see performances of classical French plays.

XXI. HISTORICAL NOTES ON THE CITY OF BASLE.

Basle was at first a Celtic settlement, then for a time a Roman camp. It became an episcopate, and, when the neighbouring town Augusta Rauracorum was destroyed by the Alemanni, Basle took its place as head of the Rauracian district; at a later period it belonged to the Carlovingian kingdom. The cathedral of Basle which had been burnt by the Hungarians, was rebuilt and liberally endowed by the Emperor Henry II. In course of time the citizens purchased from the bishops all the seignorial rights over the city and neighbourhood. As a free city of the Empire, Basle flourished by dint of trade and industry, and even a great earthquake in 1356 could not check its growth. The name of Basle was made famous by the Church Council from 1431 to 1449. One of the consequences of this ecclesiastical meeting was the foundation of the University in 1460. Soon Basle became a nursery of Humanism, and attracted the most learned scholars of that period of scientific revival.

Parallel with the flourishing of art and science printing assumed a leading part. The fame of Basle as a printing centre attracted both scholars and painters, such as Desiderius Erasmus and Hans Holbein. The unique collection of Holbein's engravings and paintings is the jewel of the Basle Art Museum. In 1501 Basle joined the Swiss Confederation. The reformation forced the bishop and chapter as well as the noble families to leave Basle for ever. French refugees who found an asylum here amply made up for the loss by starting new industries, especially the weaving of silk ribbons, which has remained one of the chief industries until this day. Ever since Basle became part of Switzerland, she was spared all wars with outward enemies. The turmoil of the French revolution and the Napoleonic wars alone caused Basle, as they did the rest of Switzerland, serious trouble. Since then Basle has enjoyed a period of almost uninterrupted peace, during which her development has gone on apace, and thanks to her favourable situation, the energy and ability of her inhabitants, she has acquired great importance as a home of industry, trade, and arts, not only for Switzerland, but for Europe in general.

XXII. A SYNOPSIS OF THE HISTORY OF THE UNIVERSITY OF BASLE.

The University of Basle, founded in 1460, is the oldest, and for 370 years was the only university in Switzerland. Its origin was due to the great Church Council which assembled at Basle from 1431 to 1449. The citizens had learnt to appreciate the value of scholarly learning, and wished to make their own town a home of learned studies. Knowing that only the Pope or the Emperor could grant the privileges for a Studium

Generale, as a University was then called, the burgomaster and aldermen of Basle applied to Pope Pius II. The Pope, when still named Enea Silvio de' Piccolomini, had been present at the Church Council for several years. (He gives a most delightful description of the town and its population in two of his letters.) Indeed, he graciously complied with the request of the Basle magistrates in a bull dated the 12th of November 1459. In this Bull the University of Basle was granted the same privileges as the University of Bologna, and the Bishops of Basle were to be its Chancellors. The University was inaugurated by a solemn Act in the Cathedral on April 4th 1460.

The History of the University may be divided into three periods, the first from its foundation to the Reformation, the second from the Reformation to the abolishment of its corporative autonomy in 1818, and the third from 1818 to the present day.

First Period, from 1460 to 1532.

The ardour with which burgomaster and aldermen had worked for the foundation of their High School was damped somewhat by the financial difficulties that arose when the Colleges had to be endowed. These difficulties were soon overcome by the generous spirit of the burghers, and by the aid of the Pope, and the University began to flourish. From the very outset she possessed four Faculties, which however, were not all on the same level, the Philosophical Faculty being then, and at a much later time, considered as a sort of preparation for the other Faculties, which were accordingly termed the Upper Faculties. Among these the Theological Faculty was placed first in rank, that of Laws second, that of Medicine third. Accordingly, a Student could not be registered in any of the Upper three Faculties, unless he had graduated in the Philosophical Faculty, or, as it was then called, Facultas Artium Liberalium.

Renaissance Chamber in Historical Museum

Wrought-iron Gate (18th century)

This is the reason why the Philosophical Faculty (corresponding to Arts and Science in a British University) is still placed last on the list, although in number and importance of disciplines as well as in the number of Students it has gained the ascendancy.

This inferiority of dignity, however, was fully compensated by the great weight which was given to the study of the chief discipline of this Faculty, Philosophy in the proper sense of the word.

Now, just at the time when the University of Basle was established, a great controversy had been started afresh between the adherents of two different schools of Philosophy, the Nominalists and the Realists. This controversy made itself felt in the first appointment of the teachers. And yet it was the professors of Philosophy that brought great credit to the University. Though the Faculty stood on the side of the Nominalists, they received among them the intrepid and energetic leader of the Realists, Johannes de Lapide (Johann Heinlin von Stein), who became in 1469 Rector of the University of Paris and Professor at the Sorbonne. Another shining light was Sebastian Brant, well known in German literature as a satiric poet.

In the front rank of the Humanists stood Glareanus (Heinrich Loriti of Glarus), Thomas Wyttenbach, the famous teacher of Zwingli and Zwingli's follower Leo Jud, and of Johannes Reuchlin, who in his turn became the teacher of Luther's helpmate Melanchthon.

The most eminent teachers in the Theological Faculty at this time were Johannes de Wesel, one of the first who attempted to reform the Church by purity of doctrine; Geiler von Keisersberg, a native of Schaffhausen, who was for more than forty years a preacher at the Strassburg Cathedral, and was reputed as the first pulpit orator of the day; Johannes Oecolampadius, who afterwards became the reformer of the Church of Basle.

The first teachers of Laws were Italians. They were succeeded in 1524 by Boniface Amerbach, the most amiable of all our Humanists. His graceful presence has been kept alive by Holbein's painting, along with that of Desiderius Erasmus, whose devoted friend he was, and whom he did not leave even on his deathbed.

As early as 1470 printing presses were set up at Basle, and turned out such splendid work that Erasmus, the greatest scholar of this period, who had been staying at Paris, London, Rome, Venice, decided to settle down at Basle. His vast learning and his urbanity soon made his house the rallying place of all that was brilliant in scholarship and wit.

At this time the Reformation took root in Basle. The religious innovations were succeeded by violent political commotions. In 1529 the reformed party gained a bloodless victory. The adherents of the Old Faith left the town, among them Erasmus and the greater part of the University professors and students.

For a time it was very doubtful whether the University would be able to survive. The remaining members of Convocation tried to take matters into their own hands by electing a new Rector. But the city magistrates, considering this as an unlawful comedy, and yet unwilling to lose the privileges of an University, seized the sceptre, seal, statute books, documents, and what was left of the treasury, implying by this action that they meant to exercise the functions hitherto vested in the Bishop and Convocation.

Second Period, from 1532 to 1818.

For three years a sort of interregnum took place. A few professors continued to hold lectures, and yet there could be no doubt that the dwindling University could no longer claim to be a legitimate Studium Generale. But however dark the prospect might be, the magistrates and citizens never for a moment entertained the thought of abandoning, for financial reasons, the palladium of their city. To rebuild the University appeared to their leaders part of the great project of making education a business of the State. They felt bound to prove to their opponents that the Protestant Church was quite as willing to patronize Science and Arts, as the Catholic Church.

As soon as the troubles of the first two religious and civil wars were over, the magistrates tried to settle the difficulty. The city government boldly assumed to itself the right of establishing a University, hitherto reserved to the Pope or Emperor. By virtue of their own authority, acting as the supreme and governing legislative body, they proclaimed the new statutes, which were sworn to by the new Rector and professors on September 20th 1532.

On November 1st letters were issued to invite Students to get enrolled on the lists of the restored University. It was to be a University of the Reformed Protestant Faith; for according to the revised statutes of July 26th 1539, no professor could be appointed, unless he was a member of the Established Church. After a period of slow recovery the University began to prosper once more.

The mainstay of the Theological Faculty in the troublous times of the Reformation was Johannes Oecolampadius (d. 1531), whose statue stands outside the cloisters of the Cathedral. Simon Sulzer (d. 1585) made an attempt to get the Established Church remodelled in conformity with the doctrines of Luther, but was defeated by J. J. Grynaeus (d. 1617). The Faculty of Laws was worthily represented by Boniface Amerbach (d. 1562) and his son Basilius Amerbach (d. 1592). Their fame does not rest on deep professional learning, but rather on their unusual civic merit. Basilius, as Syndic to the city, rendered excellent service in difficult and dangerous litigations with the Bishop. Both of them were wise and generous collectors of works of art. Their Art Cabinet was one of the nine wonders of the city to all continental tourists.

Ludwig Iselin (d. 1612), the nephew of Basilius Amerbach, who had been a student at Geneva, Bourges, Padua, and travelled far and wide, though he did not add to the literature of his profession, was so much admired as a teacher that his lectures were thronged by Students from all parts of Europe.

A brilliant representative of the French school of jurists was Francis Hotomannus (d. 1590), besides a distinguished philologist and archaeologist. His zeal for the Calvinistic doctrine made him waste his talent on theological pamphlets in the feuds of the religious parties in France.

The tradition of the Amerbachs was nobly continued by Remigius Faesch (d. 1667), whose magnificent collection was in 1823 incorporated in the University Library.

The Medical professors, Theodore Zwinger (d. 1588) and Henry Pantaleon (d. 1595), rank high among the historians and topographers of the district of Basle. Felix Platter (d. 1614), was an eminent surgeon whose services were claimed by the sovereigns of the whole continent. But his name, as well as that of his father, Thomas Platter, who from a goat-herd in the Valais rose to be the Head of the Basle Grammar School, have become illustrious in literature through their autobiographies, which, for the history of their period, hold about the same place as the Diaries of Samuel Pepys or John Evelyn for English history. Felix Platter's brother Thomas who was his junior by 38 years, was a distinguished member of the same Faculty.

As a scholar Felix Platter was surpassed by his colleague Caspar Bauhin (d. 1624), the great botanist. He was a teacher of undisputed authority, and one of the first to collect an herbarium. His Pinax Theatri Botanici, the result of forty years labour, is by experts deemed an indispensable standard work even to the modern botanist.

About this time, in the years 1542 and 1543, the greatest medical scholar of the sixteenth century, Andreas Vesalius of Brussels, stayed at Basle to supervise the printing of his Fabrica Humani Corporis. He did not enter into the Faculty, but he generously bequeathed to it the skeleton of a body he had publicly dissected. This skeleton and the one left by Felix Platter are still preserved in the Anatomical Institute, and are supposed to be the oldest specimens of the kind in any collection of Europe.

The Philosophical Faculty offered asylum to a great Italian scholar, Coelius Secundus Curio (d. 1569). He had been a professor of Laws at Milan, Pavia, and Lucca, but had been persecuted for heterodoxy. At Basle he was glad to earn his living as a professor of Rhetoric. His writings about theological, philological, antiquarian, numismatical problems show him to have been a man of unusual sagacity and versatility. As a champion of religious toleration he was seconded by the professor of Greek language, Sebastian Castellio (d. 1563), who, when at Geneva, had had a controversy with Calvin. Now, on hearing that the Spanish doctor Servetus had been burnt at the stake by the order of Calvin, he joined with Curio in denouncing this intolerant action in a pamphlet signed with the assumed name of Martinus Bellius.

It seems rather queer that another colleague, Thomas Erastus (d. 1583), though he was wise enough to ridicule the superstitious of Alchemy and Astrology, should have published a learned treatise to justify the belief in witchcraft. The same scholar gave evidence of his generous mind by bequeathing funds for a Student Scholarship.

The fame of Sebastian Münster (d. 1552) and Christian Wurstisen (d. 1588) lives down to the present day. Münster, a professor of Hebrew, and second to none but Reuchlin as a linguist, laid the foundation of the science of Comparative Geography and Ethnology by his Cosmography, which was translated into many languages and pirated by many authors.

37

Wurstisen, who was a professor of Mathematics and New Testament Theology, was holding lectures at Padua on the Copernican System when Galilei was a student there. His Chronicles of Basle (1580) were until recently highly appreciated and reprinted as most valuable contributions to local history.

In scholarly erudition they were both outdistanced by Johannes Buxtorf (d. 1629), a professor of Hebrew. Even the Jewish Talmudists acknowledged him as a first rate authority in Talmud Literature. Three of his direct descendants were highly distinguished University teachers in the same Faculty. One of the new chairs in the Theological Faculty (locorum communium atque controversiarum) was created for the purpose of binding his son Johannes to the University of Basle.

In the course of the seventeenth and eighteenth centuries the University seemed to live under a cloud. And yet even this cloud was, throughout the eighteenth century, lit up by the brilliancy of a dynasty of learned men, all belonging to one family of the town, named Bernoulli. Eight men, within three generations, were stars of the first magnitude in the domain of mathematical science. To distinguish them from each other, historians have to number them like monarchs. To some of them, Science is indebted for important discoveries and startling innovations. Jacob I invented, independently of Newton, the Calculus integralis, Johannes I discovered the Principle of Energy; he was tutor to the celebrated mathematician Leonhard Euler (d. 1780 at Petersburg), who, though not a member of Basle University, helped to support the credit of his native town. Jacob I's nephew Daniel invented Hydrodynamics, first put forward in a treatise which a modern biographer calls an immortal book.

In 1759 two friends, professors in the Theological Faculty, Johannes Ludwig Frey (d. 1759) and Johannes Grynaeus (d. 1744) founded the Frey-Grynaeus Institute for the promotion of the study of History, Classical and Oriental Languages. For this purpose they presented to it a library, containing most valuable manuscripts, incunabula, and other rare prints, among others a Second Edition of the Shakespeare Folio of 1632.

The library was constantly increased by gifts of the trustees and friends. The greater part of it was incorporated in the University Library in 1909.

The Napoleonic Era left no trace in the annals of the University. All the more important was an act of legislation in the following period.

Third Period, from 1818 to 1919.

Until now the relations between State and University had been regulated by the Statutes of 1532 and 1539, by which the University had been placed under the authority of the State; but still she had retained some rights belonging to an independent corporation. By an Act Concerning the Organisation of the University (1818) the privileges were abrogated, and the Cantonal government was made exclusively reponsible for the supervision and administration of the University. This Act was modified in 1833 after the separation of the Canton, and superseded by a new Act in 1866. A new University Organisation is under consideration, forming part of the new Educational Legislation by which the whole educational system of the city will be remodelled.

The political troubles of the year 1833, and the civil war between the capital of the Canton and the country districts resulted in a separation of the Canton into two very unequal halves. The territory of the city was reduced to its own precincts and three villages on the right bank of the Rhine. Moreover, half of the old corporation funds and endowments had to be handed over to the newly established country canton. So it was that the city, the population of which was at that time only 25,000, found itself burdened with debts, and despaired of being able to bear the expense of a University. Fortunately the generous contributions of the Academical Society, founded in 1835 by influential businessmen and men of science, encouraged the citizens to vote the funds required for the re-establishment of the University and the erection of new buildings necessitated by the growth of the Faculties and their new disciplines, especially in the departments of Medicine and Natural Science. Whenever the budget of the city was unable to bear the whole burden, grants made by the Academical Society, filled up the gaps, and enabled the University to meet with the demands made on her.

Of the University teachers appointed during this period, we will only mention those whose names will sound familiar to any one who has ever glanced at the history of learning in modern times.

In the Faculty of Theology W. de Wette, d. 1849, one of the founders of historic criticism of the Old Testament, K. R. Hagenbach, d. 1874, an eminent teacher of Church History, F. Overbeck, d. 1905, a renowned exponent of Early Christian Literature.

In the Faculty of Laws J. J. Bachofen, d. 1887, the celebrated author of the doctrine of Matriarchy.

In the Faculty of Medicine F. Miescher, d. 1895, a great author on Physiology and Histochemistry, W. His, d. 1904, a first rate authority on Embryology, M. Roth, d. 1914, best known as the biographer of Vesalius.

In the Faculty of Arts W. Wackernagel, d. 1869, one of the founders of German Philology, Jacob Burckhardt, d. 1897, a classical author on the History of Italian Art and Culture.

In the Faculty of Science C. Schönbein, d. 1868, the discoverer of ozone and inventor of gun-cotton, a friend of M. Faraday, P. Merian, d. 1883, L. Rütimeyer, d. 1895, cf. p. 27.

To those Students who come to Basle from the vast capitals of the world with High Schools endowed with millions of money by the munificence of a government or some wealthy patrons of science and arts, the buildings and rooms in which they will have to pursue their studies

Spalen Gate

Letzi-Tower. Part of Old Town-wall

at Basle, will appear rather narrow. Let them bear in mind that all the schools of Basle up to the gates of the University are free to all, Swiss and foreigners alike, and that all the costs are voted and paid by the taxpayers of one town. And these costs are borne willingly and ungrudgingly by a population to which its prosperity has not come without incessant labour.

It has been the tradition of the University of Basle to choose its teachers from among the ablest men of neighbouring countries just as well as from the ablest men of Switzerland. Many a brilliant man of science has found a second home at Basle, and has helped to cultivate the true republican spirit of humanity, toleration, independence. We trust that this spirit will remain the predominant feature of our University.

XXIII. BRITISH STUDENTS REGISTERED IN THE UNIVERSITY OF BASLE IN THE 16th, 17th, and 18th CENTURIES.

Looking over the list of Students registered in the University of Basle in the 16th and 17th centuries one is struck by a goodly number of British names that sound very familiar to the lover of British history. Of the twenty-seven British students, for instance, who were entered in the University register in 1554, 1555, and 1556, more than half were afterwards distinguished either as statesmen or divines.

Sir Francis Walsingham was Secretary of State to Queen Elizabeth. Sir Francis Knollys, through his wife related to Queen Elizabeth, was one of the Keepers of Mary Queen of Scots. Anthony Denney and his brothers Henry and Charles were sons of Sir Anthony Denney, a favourite of Henry VIII. John Bale, bilious Bale, Bishop of Ossory, had two of his works printed at Basle, two others at Zurich and Geneva. John Fox, the great martyriologist, found employment here at the printing-office of Hans Herbster, or Oporinus, who edited for him, besides two minor books, the original Latin version of the Acts and Monuments of Protestant English Martyrs. Thomas Bentham was Bishop of Lichfield and Coventry. James Pilkington was the first Protestant Bishop of Durham. Peter Morwen was a Prebendary of Papa Minor in Lichfield Cathedral Laurence Humphrey, the Papistomastix, was Dean of Gloucester and Winchester, and Regius Professor of Divinity in the University of Oxford. Anthony Gilby was Vicar of Ashby de la Zouch. Christopher Goodman was the lifelong friend of John Knox and helped Coverdale in translating the Bible. Augustine Bradbridge was Treasurer and Prebendary of Fordingdon in the Diocese of Sarum. All the twenty-seven seem to have been martyrs of their religious convictions; they left England for the continent on the accession of Queen Mary, and returned shortly before, or after her death. Some twenty years later Laurence Bodley, Canon of Exeter, and his brother, Sir Thomas Bodley, founder of the Bodleian Library, resided at Basle. Even an American Indian, named Didacus Lainus, found his way to Basle in 1585.

The queer spelling of some of the names in the list given below may be owing to clerical errors of the copyist.

1541 Richardus Eckundus Anglus

1554 Petrus Morwingus Anglus (P. Morwen, 1530 ?-1573, Rector of Langwith, Norbury, Ryton, Prebendary of Papa Minor in Lichfield Cathedral.

Gabriel Poines Anglus

Richardus Bunnus Anglus

Augustinus Bradbrydge Anglus (A. Bradbridge, Prebendary of Fordingdon, Diocese of Sarum, in 1556)

Christophorus Goodmannus Anglus, Cestrensis (C. Goodman, 1520 ?-1603, joined John Knox at Edinburgh, after his return to England he lived privately at Chester)

Adamus Hallidutz Anglus Northumbrensis

1555 Anthonius Denneius nobilis ex Anglia

Henricus Denneius nobilis ex Anglia

Carolus Denneius nobilis ex Anglia (sons of Sir Anthony Denney, 1501-1549, favourite of King Henry VIII)

Franciscus Walsinghamus nobilis ex Anglia (Sir Francis Walsingham, 1530 ?-1590, Ambassador in France and Secretary of State to Queen Elizabeth)

Guilielmus Templeus Anglus

Jacobus Bantus Anglus

Dominus Johannes Baleus Anglus quondam episcopus Ossoriensis in Hybernia (J. Bale, 1495-1563, Bishop of Ossory in 1552, died as a Prebendary at Canterbury)

Anthonins Gylbaeus Anglus (A. Gilby, d. 1585, Pastor of the English Congregation at Geneva, Vicar of Ashby de la Zouch)

Alexander Cogburnus Scotus

Johannes Stantonus Anglus

Rogerus Relke Anglus

Thomas Benthannus Anglus (T. Bentham, 1513-1578, Preacher to the Exiles at Basle, appointed Bishop of Lichfield and Coventry in 1559)

Laurentius Homphredus Anglus (L. Humphrey, D. D. 1527 ?-1590, Regius Professor of Divinity at Oxford, a fervent Calvinist)

1556 Johannes Foxus Anglus exul (John Fox, 1516-1587, author of the Book of Martyrs)

Franciscus Knolleus Anglus (Sir Francis Knollys, 1514 ?-1596, statesman, very intimate with Edward VI and Princess Elizabeth, Governor of Portsmouth, controller of Sidney's expedition to Ireland, joint-controller of Mary Queen of Scots)

Richardus Springham Anglus

Johannes Bartholomeus Anglus

Jacobus Pilkington Anglus (Dr J. Pilkington, 1520 ?-1576, first Protestant Bishop of Durham)

Guilielmus Amundesam Anglus

Johannes Andlaeus Anglus

Johannes Dodmanus Anglus

1557 Oct. 8: Rupertus Herlesdonus Anglus

Oct. 15: Georgius Sefoldus Anglus

Nov. 17: Michael Levus ex Barthen Anglus

Dec. 10: Christopherus Suthesus Anglus

1558 Mai. 12: Johannes Blochus Anglus

Mai. 20: Thomas Stuardus Anglus

Robertus Horn Anglus (R. Horn, 1519 ?-1580, Chaplain to Edward VI, Dean of Durham, Prebendary of Bugthorpe in York Minster, Bishop of Winchester in 1560, D. D. Oxford 1568)

Anthonins Mayhewe Anglus

1560 Guilielmus Clerus Cantabrigensis Anglus

Guilielmus Tendalus Anglus

Johannes Tendalus Anglus

Henricus Tendalus Anglus

Ambrosius Germinus Anglus

1571 Dominus Richardus Deilior Anglus

1575 Laurentius Badleus Anglus (L. Bodley, d. 1615, Canon of Exeter, brother of Sir Thomas Bodley)

Johannes Davidsonius Scotus (J. Davidson, 1549 ?-1603, great preacher, favourite with King James VI)

1576 Robertus Jacob Londinensis Anglus (R. Jacob, d. 1588, Physician to Queen Elizabeth)

Edoardus Untonus Anglus

Henricus Untonus Anglus (Sir Henry Unton, 1557 ?-1596, Ambassador to Henry IV in France)

Johannes Delaberus Anglus

Johannes Ashfildus Anglus

Thomas Cartwrightus Anglus (T. Cartwright, 1535-1563, a learned Puritan Divine)

1578 Apr. 13: Thomas Moufetus Londinus Anglus (T. Moffett, 1553-1604, physician and author, supporter of the Paracelsian system)

1578 Oct. 11: Thomas Baedleus nobilis Oxoniensis Anglus (Sir Thomas Bodley, 1545-1613, founder of Bodleian Library)

Anthonins Honoratus Florentinus ipsius famulus

Guilielmus Gent Oxoniensis nobilis Anglus

1579 Dominus Franciscus Hastingus filius fratris comitis Kindgoviae Anglus

Ricardus Polaeus Anglus

1580 Thomas Goccheus Anglus

1580 Aug.: Johannes Craygus Scotus (J. Craig, d. 1620, Physician to James VI)

1580 Oct.: Stephanus Polus Anglus

Robertus Nulcomen Anglus

1580 Nov.: Guilielmus Andersonius Scotus

1581 Jan.: Henricus ab Hastings Anglus

Thomas Church Anglus

1581 Jun.: Henricus Baringtonus Cantabrigensis

Thomas Doyleus Oxoniensis (T. D'Oylie, M.D., 1543 ?-1613, Spanish scholar)

Tertullianus Pynns Oxoniensis

Thomas Burlaeus Cantabrigensis

Guilielmus Bugginus Londinensis

Emanuel Barneus palatini Dunelmensis filius Anglus

Hilarius Fautrartus ex insula Gernesea Anglus

1582 Johannes Morus Anglus

1584 Apr.: Johannes Sieddus Londinensis Anglus
Simeon Randallus Anglus
1584 Aug.: Guilielmus Papius Aberdonensis Scotus
1584 Sept. : Magister Thomas Hauwes Cantabrigensis Anglus
1585 Oct.: Edmundus Brucins Anglus nobilis
Eduardus Seluinus Anglus nobilis
Wilhelmus Lovius Scotus
Didacus Lainus Americus Indus
1586 Mai.: Carolus Merburgius Anglus nobilis (Charles Merbury ?, an
agent of Sir Francis Walsingham in France)
1587 Oct.: Eduardus Zoutheus nobilis Anglus
Guilielmus Vuardus Anglus
Henricus Hakinsus Anglus
1588 Apr.: Eduardus Jorden ex Cantia Anglus (E. Jorden, M. D., 1560-
1632, Physician, and Chemist)
1588 Mai.: Robertus Houaeus Scotus
1592 Thomas Pato Saxomedius Anglus
Fynes Morison Anglus
1592 Sept.: Magister Jacobus Cargyllus Aberdonensis Scotus (J. Cargill,
Botanist, aided Bauhin and Gesner in their collections and writings)
1595 Jacobus Medousius Anglocestrensis
1596 Rogerus Andertonus Anglus
Guilielmus Clemens Anglus
Josephus Lister Anglus
1599 Sept.: Simeon Rutingius Anglus
1599 Oct.: Tobias Albins Londinensis
1600 Apr.: Novellus de Sparke Anglus
1601 Jun. 5: Thomas Mortonius Edimburgensis Scotus
1604 Nov.: Guilielmus Sheianus Hibernus
1605 Mart.: Magister Patricius Kynnerus Scotus

1605 Petrus Mousellus Anglus

1607 Magister Guilielmus Kragius Scotus
Patricius Doneus Scotus

1608 Apr.: Laurentius Carleil Londinensis Anglus

1608 Mai.: Magister David Narneus Andreapolitanus Scotus
Magister Guilielmus Forbesius Abredonensis Scotus (W. Forbes,
1585-1634, first bishop of Edinburgh)

1608 Nov.: Jacobus Hartus Scotus (J. Hart, physician and author, North-
ampton)

1609 Mart.: Arthurus Dee Anglus Mortlake (A. Dee, 1579-1651, Alchemist,
Physician to the Tsar and to Charles I)
Richardus Mylnes Anglo-Britannus Londinensis

1610 Mai.: Jacobus Tough Scoto-Britannus

1610 Jul.: Magister Johannes Leslaeus Scoto-Britannus (J. Leslie, 1571-
1671, Bishop of Clogher, stout royalist)

1613 Mai.: Paulus Peneus Londinensis

1613 Dec.: Magister Jacobus Forbesius Corsindacus Scotus

1615 Apr.: Franciscus Carcio (Coccio?) Anglus
Thomas Walkeden Anglus

1616 Jan.: Gregorius Wright Anglus

1616 Febr.: Thomas Cumin Scoto-Belga

1620 Febr.: Patricius Falconatus Merniensis Scotus

1625 Jul.: Thomas Lindeseus Scotus Edimburgensis

1631 Febr.: Basilius Vicecomes Fillding Anglus (Basil Feilding, 2nd Earl
of Denbigh, d. 1675, leader of Parliamentary army)
Robertus Mason Anglus
Balthasarus Grieneroaye (sic) Anglus
Georgius Lyddier Anglus

1633 Mart.: Nathanael a Fiennes nobilis Anglus (N. Fiennes, 1608 ?-1669, 2nd son of William, 1st Viscount Say and Sele, Commander and Parliamentarian)
Josephus a Fiennes nobilis Anglus (J. Fiennes, 3rd son of William, 1st Viscount Say and Sele, Commander and Parliamentarian)
Joannes a Fiennes nobilis Anglus

1633 Carolus Cottrel Anglus (Sir Charles Cotterell, 1615-1687, Master of Ceremonies to Charles I and Charles II)
Guillelmus Ball Hibernus
Carolus Riche de Warwick nobilis Anglus
Henricus Riche de Warwick nobilis Anglus (H. Rich, Earl of Holland, 1590-1649, 2nd son of Robert, 1st Earl of Warwick. James I's agent in France for the marriage of Prince Charles and Princess Henrietta Maria of France; beheaded 1649)

1635 Aug.: Guilielmus Mancknoull Anglus Eboracensis

1640 Georgius Clark Scoto-Britannus

1645 Alexander Junius Scoto-Britannus

1647 Ropertus Napier Anglus
Richardus Rencius Anglus
Robertus Daulinus Edimburgensis Scotus

1663 Dec. 19: Johannes Anglesius Anglus

1666 Mai. 17: William Hastinges Anglus

1669 Sept. 30: Patricius Shau Scotus

1671 Nov. 24: Patricius Molineus Scotus

1672 Oct. 15: Franciscus Tallents Anglus (F. Tallents, 1619-1668, ejected Divine)
Jacobus Disleo Anglus

1702 Sept. 30: Johannes Mack Gregory Scotus Edimburgensis

1705 Dec. 10: Jenkinus Thomasius Anglus

1711 Oct. 17: Johannes Arnoldus Exonio-Anglus

Angenstein Castle near Basle

Pfeffingen Castle near Basle

1714 Jun. 5: Henricus Leslie Hibernus
1716 Dec. 15: Henricus Gaile Londinensis
1732 Mai. 15: James Perchard Angleterre
1734 Aug. 10: John Goodwyn Dublinensis
1737 Oct. 17: Guilielmus Codringtonus Eques Anglicus
1750 Mai. 20: Johannes Hennessy de Halley ex Bedfordshire
1771 Oct. 22: William Samson Anglus

XXIV. SURVEY OF THE COURSES OF INSTRUCTION.

A. Faculty of Theology.

The University confers the degree of Licentiate of Theology quali-fying for academic teaching.

Within two academic years, or four semesters, lectures and Seminar Exercises, are held, in regular rotation. These cover the whole ground of the Theological disciplines that have to be gone through by Swiss Grad-uate Students of the Reformed Protestant Church. As most of the Lect-ures are held by two Professors in the same term, Students are certain to hear all the problems of Theological Science dealt with by men representing different schools and views.

Every fourth semester an Introductory Lecture on the Encyclopaedia of Theology is held by Prof. E. Vischer.

1. General History of Religious.
   Prof. B. Duhm, Prof. A. Alt.
   Besides the lectures on the General History of Religions, Lectures on all the Historic Phenomena bearing on the History of the New Test-ament are held by exponents of the New Testament.

Non-Christian religions are also discussed from the philosophical point of view by the teachers of Systematic Theology.

2. Old Testament Exegesis.
Prof. B. Duhm, Prof. A. Alt.
Introductory Lectures and Seminar Exercises on all the chief books of the Old Testament, on the History of Israel, on the History of Old Testament Religion, Exercises in Hebrew Grammar and Literature for Beginners and Advanced Students.

3. New Testament Exegesis.
Prof. K. Goetz, Prof. E. Riggenbach.
Lectures and Seminar Exercises on all the chief books of the New Testament, on New Testament Theology (Religion and Ethics of Primitive Christianity), on the Problems of the Life of Christ, on St. Paul and the Apostolic Age, on the Historic Phenomena of the New Testament World.

New Testament research being the central and radiating point of Theological study, all the Professors of Church History and Systematic Theology will deal with the Problems of New Testament History.

4. Church History.
Prof. P. Wernle, Prof. E. Vischer, Prof. P. Böhringer.
Lectures and Seminar Exercises on the History of Early Christianity, Greek and Latin Christianity, History of Church Reformation, History of Modern Religious Thought, History of Dogma, Theology of the Reformed Protestant Faith.

Lectures on Symbolics (History of Confessions), Theology of Protestantism and representative leaders of the Protestant Church are held by the Professors of Systematic Theology as well.

Special Lectures and Exercises on important personalities and Problems of Church History by E. Stähelin, L. Th.

5. Systematic Theology.

Prof. J. Wendland, Prof. G. Heinzelmann.

Lectures and Seminar Exercises on Christian Dogmatics. Part. I. Principles of Religion, Philosophy of Religion, Christian Apologetics. Part II. Principles of Christianity and its Evolution, Christian Ethics and Symbolics.

Special Problems and Readings. K. Zickendraht, L. Th.

6. Practical Theology.

Prof. R. Handmann.

Lectures on the Tasks of the Christian Ministry, Forms of Worship, Theory and Practice of Homiletics, Tasks of Religious Education.

J. Frohnmeyer, D. D., late Inspector of African Missions, will introduce Students into all the aspects and problems of foreign mission work and practical missionary service.

All Students have free access to the Theological Reference Library which is being constantly added to and brought up to date.

B. Faculty of Laws.

The University confers the Degree of Doctor of Laws (Juris Utriusque Doctor). The chief lectures are repeated every two or four semesters.

1. Civil Law.

Prof. K. Wieland, Prof. F. Beyerle, Prof. A. Simonius.

Lectures on the New Swiss Code of Civil Law (which came into force on Jan. 1st 1912, the most progressive of continental codes, dealing with Law of Persons and Families, Inheritance, Property), on the Swiss Law of Contracts and Liability (enacted 1881, revised 1912).

Prof. K. Wieland, joint author of Codification of Swiss Civil Law and Law of Contracts. Special Lectures on Laws of Commerce, Copyright, Patent, Exchange, Insurance.

Dr F. Goetzinger, President of the High Court of Appeal. Special Lectures on problems of Swiss Civil Law.

Dr M. Stähelin. Special Lectures on Accountancy, Banking.

2. History of Legislation.

Prof. A. Simonius.

History of Roman Law, Institutions, Pandects. Lectures and Interpretation of Passages of Digests and other Sources of Roman Law.

Prof. K. Beyerle, Dr Henrici, Dr J. Wackernagel.

Special Lectures and Practical Courses in History of German Law, History of Swiss Civil Law, Interpretation of German and Swiss legal Documents.

The Law Section of the University Library is unusually rich in old collections of German and Italian documents relating to Municipal Legislation, moreover in rare collections of Manuscript Digests with Commentaries by Bologna Scholars and old editions of such Commentaries. The Municipal Archives contain the most complete Collection of Transactions of Law-suits dating from the early Middle Ages.

3. Criminal Law, Law of Evidence, Civil Procedure.

Prof. A. Schoetensack.

A new Swiss Code of Criminal Law is under consideration.

4. Constitutional and Administrative Legislation, International Law.

Prof. E. Ruck, Dr E. His.

Swiss Federal Constitution, Modern Social Legislation, Canonical Law (Interpretation of the new Codex Juris Canonici).

5. Philosophy of Law.

Prof. A. Schoetensack.

Students of Law have free access to all Courts of Law, the transactions of wich very frequently bear on interesting topics of International Law.

Five of the teachers in this Faculty are members of the High Court of Appeal. Two professors, A. Heusler and P. Speiser, who are still members of the Faculty, and who combine high scholarship with splendid practical legislative activity, are well known to the learned world as first rate authorities in matters of practical jurisprudence.

Economics and Statistics.

According to old usage still incorporated in Faculty of Philosophy All the disciplines of this Section are represented so fully that Students are certain to get acquainted with all the views and doctrines of modern teachers of Laws and Economics.

Prof. J. Landmann. Lectures on Principles of Economics, Banking, Insurance, Credit, Seminar for Research-Students.

Prof. R· Michels. Lectures on Theory of National Economy, and History, Statistics of Administration, Problems of Party Politics and Social Psychology, Seminar for Research-Students.

Prof. St· Bauer. Lectures on the same disciplines, including Currency and Banking, Seminar for Research-Students.

Dr L. Furlan. Theory of Statistics, Agrarian Economy, Practical Courses in Statistics.

C. Faculty of Medicine.

The University confers the Degree of Doctor of Medicine, Surgery, and Obstetrics. It comprises all the Courses of Instruction necessary for the theoretical training of physicians and surgeons. The teaching staff consists of 13 Professors ordinarii, 8 Professors extraordinarii, 24 Privatdozenten, besides a large number of assistants, demonstrators etc. The Medical Institutes are equipped with the latest appliances.

1. Anatomical Institute (Vesalianum).

Prof. H. Corning, with a Professor extraord. and a Prosector.

Lectures and Practical Courses in Descriptive and Topographical Anatomy, Embryology, Histology.

2. Physiological Institute.

Prof. G. von Bunge, Prof. R. Metzner, with assistants.

Lectures and Practical Courses in Experimental Physiology, Laboratory-work.

3. Pharmacological Institute.

Prof. A. Jaquet, with assistants.

Lectures on Pharmacology, Experimental Pathology and Therapy. New buildings are being erected for the three Institutes.

4. Institute for Pathological Anatomy, in a special wing of the Municipal Hospital.

Prof. E. Hedinger, with assistants.

Lectures on General Pathology, Practical Courses in Dissection.

5. Institute for Bacteriology and Hygiene.

Prof. A. Burckhardt, with assistants.

Lectures on General Hygiene, Public Health Legislation, Factory and School Hygiene, Practical Courses in Methods of bacteriological and serological investigation. In summer outdoor instruction in Private and Public Hygiene.

6. Medical Clinic in the Municipal Hospital.

Prof. R. Stähelin, with 2 Professors extraord., 2 Privatdozenten, 11 assistants, 6 subassistants. Under his superintendançe are wards with several hundred beds, large laboratories, an Institute for Physico-Therapeutics, Isolation wards for Infectious Diseases, and a Suburban Convalescent Home.

7. Surgical Clinic.

Prof. R. Hotz, with 12 assistants.

Extensive In and Out-Patient Departments, with Röntgen Cabinets. Particular attention is given to Treatment of Factory Accidents for which there is a special teacher and a privatdozent.

8. Laryngological Clinic.

Prof. F. Siebenmann, with assistants and demonstrators.

Lectures and Practical Courses.

9. Dermatological Clinic.

Prof. F. Lewandowsky, with assistants.

Departments for In and Out-Patients.

Lectures and Practical Courses in Dermatology and Diseases of the Genital Organs.

10. University Policlinic for Interior Medicine.

Prof. F. Egger, with assistants.

Gratuitous consultations for Out-Patients from City and Neighbourhood.

11. Municipal Women's Hospital.

Is generally acknowledged to be a model institution of its kind.

Prof. A. Labhardt with a Professor extraord., 2 Privatdozenten, 5 assistant surgeons.

Clinical Lectures and Practical Courses in Midwifery and Gynaecology.

12. Ophthalmic Hospital.

Prof. A. Vogt with 4 Privatdozenten, Departments for In and Out-Patients. Lectures and Practical Courses in Diseases of the Eye.

13. Cantonal Asylum for the Treatment of the Insane.

Prof. G. Wolff with numerous assistants. Lectures and Demonstrations on Mental Diseases.

14. Children's Hospital and Policlinic.

Prof. E. Wieland with numerous assistants. Departments for In and Out-Patients. Lectures and Demonstrations on Children's Diseases.

15. A number of Private Hospitals, conducted by University Professors and Privatdozenten, offer courses of instruction in Special Diseases of the Digestive Organs, Diseases of the Throat, Ear, Eye etc., as well as courses of instruction in Surgery.

16. Besides the Lectures and Practical Courses mentioned above, there are Lectures held on Forensic Medicine, Forensic Psychiatry, Climato-Balneo-Therapy, Medical Statistics, History of Medicine, Medical Ethics, Social Hygiene, Biological Psychology etc.

In all the Institutes of the Faculty of Medicine Graduate and Postgraduate Students will find every facility for independent research-work and preparing Theses.

Foreign Graduate and Postgraduate Students who have given sufficient proof of their qualifications may be elected as paid or unpaid assistants. All the Institutes have well-stocked reference libraries and reading-rooms with free access to all registered students.

D. Faculty of Arts (Faculty of Philosophy, First Section).

The University confers the Degree of Ph. D. (Philosophiae Doctor).

1. Philosophy.

Prof. K. Joël, Privatdozent W. von Olshausen.

Roman Theatre at Augst near Basle

Courtyard in Historical Museum

Introductory Lectures on Psychology, Logic and Ethics, History of Philosophy Ancient and Modern, Reading of standard-works with discussions.

2. Principles of Comparative Philology and Oriental Languages.

Prof. M. Niedermann, Prof. J. Wackernagel, Prof. F. Schulthess.

Introductory Lectures on the Principles of Comparative Philology, Special Problems of Aryan Languages, Interpretation of Indian, Iranian Greek, Latin, Romanic, Baltic, Slavic Texts. Lectures and Exercises on Semitic Languages and Problems of Mohammedan Religion.

3. Classical Philology.

Prof. J. Wackernagel, Prof. J. Stroux, Prof. P. VonderMühll, Prof. M. Niedermann.

Lectures on Comparative History of Classical Languages. History of Greek and Roman Literature. Greek and Latin Palaeography and Criticism. Interpretation of Greek and Latin texts. Greek and Latin Composition. Seminar exercises.

4. Classical Archaeology.

Prof. E. Pfuhl.

Lectures on History of Greek and Roman Art and Archaeology. Demonstrations in Museums and Sculpture Hall.

Students of Archaeology will be interested in the ruins of a Roman garrison town, Augusta Rauracorum (6 miles to the East of Basle), founded by Munatius Plancus at the same time with Lugdunum or Lyons, and in a fine collection of Roman antiquities in the Historical Museum.

5. German Philology.

Prof. E. Hoffmann-Krayer, Prof. W. Bruckner. Old German Grammar and Texts. German Phonetics.

Prof. F. Zinkernagel, History of Modern German Literature.

Dr M. Nussberger. History of German Swiss Literature.

Prof. E. Hoffmann-Krayer. History of Swiss Dialects, Swiss Folk Lore, with Demonstrations in Swiss Ethnological Museum.

6. Romanic Philology.

Prof. E. Tappolet, History of French Literature, French and Romanic Grammar. History of Swiss Patois. French Phonetics.

Dr H. Matthey. Exercises in French Grammar and Composition, Readings.

Prof. E. Walser. History of Italian Literature. Special Problems of Italian Humanism.

Dr E. Janner. Exercises in Italian Grammar and Composition, Readings.

7. English Philology.

Prof. H. Hecht. History of Old, Middle, Modern English Literature and Language.

Dr K. Jost. English Phonetics. English Syntax. Exercises in Old English.

8. History.

Prof. A. Baumgartner. Ancient Greek and Roman History.

Prof. F. Stähelin. History of the Orient. Problems of Greek Constitutional and Political History.

Prof. R. Thommen. Swiss History up to the French Revolution. Practical Courses in Palaeography.

Prof. H. Bächtold. History of Civilisation. History of Trade and Commerce. Political and Economic History of Switzerland.

Prof. E. Dürr. History of the 15th and 16th centuries.

Prof. A. Baumgartner. Prof. J. Schneider. History of the Napoleonic Age. History of the 19th century.

Dr F. Vischer. Modern Swiss History.

Prof. J. Schneider. Methods of Teaching History.

9. History of Art.

Prof. F. Rintelen. General History of Art. The Age of Renaissance.

Prof. P. Ganz. The Age of Barocco and Rococo. History of Swiss Art.

Prof. E. Stückelberg. Historic Monuments of Switzerland.

10. History and Theory of Music.

Prof. K. Nef. Dr K. Gerold.

E. Faculty of Science (Faculty of Philosophy, Second Section).

The University confers the Degree of Doctor of Philosophy, equivalent to Doctor of Science.

To the Institutes of this Faculty not only matriculated Students are admitted, but also other persons wishing to pursue a certain course of experimental and research work, provided they have satisfied the Professors in charge of the Instruction Courses as to their qualification for such work.

Mathematics, Physics, Chemistry.

1. Mathematical Institute.

There is a Seminar for Pure Mathematics and another for Mathematical Physics.

Prof. W. Matthies. Prof. H. Mohrmann. Prof. O. Spiess.

a) Pure Mathematics.

Introductory Lectures on Differential and Integral Calculus. Lectures on Analytical Geometry, Algebraic Analysis, Descriptive Geometry, Theory of Functions, Elliptic Functions, Differentiation and Integration of Functions. Geometry of Surfaces etc.

Alternative Lectures on Problems of Geometry, Calculus of Variations, Theory of Numbers, Theory of Quantics etc.

Prof. O. Spiess, History of Mathematics.

Specialists for this discipline will find invaluable materials in the Mathematical Section of the University Library. The Pedagogy of Mathematics is taught by the Headmaster of the Upper Real School, Dr R. Flatt.

b) Mathematical Physics.

Principles of Mathematical Physics. Mechanics. Analytical Method of Natural Science. Theory of Elasticity. Electromagnetic Theory of Light and Theory of Heat. Theory of Physical Instruments.

2. Institute of Astronomy and Meteorology.

Prof. Th. Niethammer. Lectures and Practical Courses in Spherical Astronomy, Measurement of Space and Time, Methods of Determining Geographical Position, Use of Astronomical Instruments.

For advanced Students: Theory of Celestial Motion, Theory of Aberration. Measurement by Pendulum, Clock, Chronograph etc.

Dr M. Knapp. Lectures on Popular Astronomy. Reading of old Authors on Astronomy.

3. Physical Institute.

Prof. A. Hagenbach. Lectures and Demonstrations on Experimental Physics, Spectroscopy. Modern Problems of Physics. Research-work.

Prof. H. Veillon. Lectures on Theory of Gases, Thermo-Dynamics, Interference, Manual Training for Research-Students.

Prof. H. Zickendraht. Lectures on Aerodynamics, Aeronautics, Electrical Technology, Radiotelegraphy, Scientific Photography, Practical Course in Electrotechnics.

Prof. L. Zehnder. Lectures on History of Physics.

Practical Courses in Laboratory Work by the first three Professors jointly.

4. Pharmaceutical Institute.

Prof. H. Zörnig. Lectures and Demonstrations on Anatomy and Physiology of Medicinal Plants, Methods of Microscopical Analysis, Pharmacological Chemistry.

Dr P. Fleissig. Special Courses in Laboratory Work. Preparation of Drugs and Medicines. Microscopical Examination of Drugs.

5. Institute for Analytical Chemistry.

Prof. H. Kreis, Cantonal Analytical Chemist. Lectures and Practical Courses in Analysis of Food-stuffs.

6. Institute for Organic and Inorganic Chemistry.

a) Prof. H. Rupe and assistants. Section for Organic Chemistry.

b) Prof. F. Fichter and assistants. Section for Inorganic Chemistry.

Lectures on Synthetical Chemistry. Experimental Chemistry of Compounds of Carbon.

Lectures on Analytical and Inorganical Chemistry chiefly to suit the requirements of Students of Medicine and Pharmacology; Electro-Chemistry, Inorganic Experimental Chemistry, Chemistry of Colloids.

Special Lectures on the Derivatives of Benzol are held with a view to train specialists for the most important branch of Basle Industries, the manufacture of aniline dyes.

The same tendency of adapting scientific research work to the requirements of Science as applied in the local industries prevails in the Practical Work of the Laboratory Courses.

7. Institute for Physical Chemistry.

Prof. A. Bernoulli and assistants. Lectures on the Principles of Chemistry, Electrolysis, Kinetics of Reaction, Problems of Metallurgy, Photochemistry, Kinetic Theory of Matter. Practical and Research-work.

Special Courses in Thermo-chemical and Electro-chemical Measurement, Optical Methods of Chemistry.

Natural Science.

The immediate vicinity of the City of Basle, especially toward the North, is characterized by the diluvial deposits of the Rhine and its affluents. To the South the City borders on the Jura range, distinguished for its calcareous alpine formation, its steep cliffs, rugged glens and valleys, its folding and arching stratification. To the North it borders on the Black-Forest, made up of primitive rock, Granite and Gneiss, offering abundant material not only to the Petrographer, Mineralogist, and Geographer, but to the Zoologist as well. Similar to the Black-Forest in their composition, but with their carboniferous strata lying more open to view, are the Vosges to the North-West of Basle.

Within a day's journey is the Kaiserstuhl, an extinct volcano, interesting for its xerophilous flora. No end of problems are offered by the Alpine ranges with their snows and glaciers; they are made easily accessible by mountain railways and good hotel accommodation.

1. Institute for Mineralogy and Petrography.

Prof. C. Schmidt, Prof. H. Preiswerk, and assistants.

Lectures and Demonstrations on Mineralogy and Crystallography, Practical Applications of Geology.

2. Institute for Geology and Palaeontology.

Prof. A. Buxtorf and assistants.

Lectures and Demonstrations on Geology, Characters of Fossils.

Regular excursions for outdoor research into the four neighbouring mountain ranges.

3. Zoological Institute.

Prof. F. Zschokke, with a Privatdozent and assistants.

Lectures, Demonstrations and Repetition-Courses in General Zoology, Systematic Zoology, Comparative Anatomy of Vertebrates and Invertebrates. Practical Courses of Dissection and Microscopical Study in the Zootomical Laboratory for Beginners and Advanced Students. Regular Excursions for outdoor research.

Dr N. Lebedinsky, Special Lectures on Biology of Vertebrates, Sexual Dimorphism, Comparative and Experimental Embryology.

In the past years advanced Students have carried on extensive investigations in the Swiss lakes and rivers from a faunistical, helminthological, and hydrobiological point of view.

The Zoological Gardens of Basle (the only ones in Switzerland) are a useful addition to the materials of the Zoological Institute.

4. Botanical Institute and Gardens.

Prof. G. Senn and assistants.

Lectures and Demonstrations on Anatomy and Physiology of Plants, Systematic Botany, Physiology of Alpine Plants, Tropical Plants, Palaeophytology.

Lectures and Demonstrations on Morphology of Plants, Pharmacological Botany, Problems of Evolution.

Practical Courses in Microscopical Research, Determination of Cryptogams and Phanerogams.

Regular excursions with Field Classes.

Particular stress is laid on the investigation of Flagellates and Algae, Anatomical and Physiological investigations of Phanerogams.

For research-work in Alpine Botany there is a special laboratory in the Engadine situated at a height of 2450 m. (8130 feet.)

5. Geographical Institute.

Prof. H. Hassinger, with assistants.

Lectures and Demonstrations on General Geography, Regional Geography, Swiss Regional Geography, Economical and Political Geography. Anthropology.

6. Ethnology.

Prof. F. Speiser.

Lectures and Demonstrations in General and Detailed Ethnography. The Ethnological Museum supplying the materials for demonstration and research-work is most remarkable for the Collections from the Malayan Archipelago and Melanesia.

❖　❖　❖

For further information foreign Students are requested to apply to the University Registrar (Pedell der Universität Basel).

❖　❖　❖

CPSIA information can be obtained
at www.ICGtesting.com
Printed in the USA
BVHW071627280119
538839BV00028B/2189/P